Amazing You

Graphology

Teresa Moorey

h

a division of Hodder Headline Limited

Sharp writing for smart people

Welcome to *AMAZING YOU - GRAPHOLOGY*

Discover what your handwriting reveals about you with the help of this *Amazing You* title.

Also available are *Astrology, Dreams, Face and Hand Reading, Numerology, Psychic Powers* and *Spells* – there are more to come in the *Amazing You* series and you can be the first to discover them!

BITE HERE!

Wanna join the gang? All the latest news, gossip and prize giveaways from BITE! **PLUS** more information on new titles in the *Amazing You* series.

Sign up NOW to join the BITE gang, and get a limited edition denim BITE bag or an exclusive preview copy of a brand new teen title, long before it's available in the shops.

To sign up text WRITING to 60022

or go to **www.bookswithbite.co.uk**

WIN! Writing love letters will never be the same again! By texting WRITING to 60022, you will automatically be entered into the draw to win a fantastic writing set. So get texting ...

Texting costs your normal rate, texts from Bite are free.
You can unsubscribe at any time by texting BITE STOP.
Terms & Conditions Apply. For details go to www.bookswithbite.co.uk

About the series

Amazing You is our stunning new Mind Body Spirit
series. It shows you how to make the most of your life
and boost your chances of success and happiness.
You'll discover some fantastic things about you and
your friends by trying out the great tips and fun
exercises. See for yourself just how amazing you
can be!

Available now
Astrology
Dreams
Face and Hand Reading
Graphology
Numerology
Psychic Powers
Spells

Coming soon
Crystals
Fortune Telling

About the author

Teresa Moorey is a counsellor, astrologer and author of over forty books on witchcraft and related subjects. She is also a mother of four children aged 6–23. Teresa writes for *Mizz* magazine and *Here's Health*, and is the author of *Spell Bound: The Teenage Witch's Essential Wicca Handbook* and *Witchcraft: A Beginner's Guide*. She has written *Crystals, Fortune Telling, Graphology* and *Spells* in the *Amazing You* series.

Text copyright © Teresa Moorey 2004
Illustrations copyright © Jo Quinn/Inkshed.co.uk 2004
Cover illustration © Monica Laita 2004

Editor: Katie Sergeant
Book design by Don Martin
Cover design: Hodder Children's Books

Published in Great Britain in 2004
by Hodder Children's Books

The right of Teresa Moorey to be identified as the author of this Work
and Jo Quinn as the illustrator of this Work has been asserted by them
in accordance with the Copyright, Designs and Patents Act 1988.

All rights reserved. Apart from any use permitted under UK copyright
law, this publication may only be reproduced, stored or transmitted, in
any form, or by any means with prior permission in writing of the
publishers or in the case of reprographic production in accordance with
the terms of licences issued by the Copyright Licensing Agency.

A catalogue record for this book is available from the British Library.

10 9 8 7 6 5 4 3 2 1

ISBN: 0340883677

Printed and bound by Bookmarque Ltd, Croydon, Surrey

The paper and board used in this paperback by Hodder Children's Books
are natural recyclable products made from wood grown in sustainable
forests. The manufacturing processes conform to the environmental
regulations of the country of origin.

Hodder Children's Books
a division of Hodder Headline Limited
338 Euston Road, London NW1 3BH

Contents

Introduction   *ix*

Chapter one: *Secrets of graphology*   *1*

Chapter two: *Pen pals*   *19*

Chapter three: *Love letters*   *31*

Chapter four: *Family A B C*   *39*

Chapter five: *Your talents in your writing*   *52*

Chapter six: *Putting on the style*   *61*

Chapter seven: *How confident are you?*   *67*

Chapter eight: *Writing in colour*   *80*

Chapter nine: *Properly addressed*   *87*

Chapter ten: *How do you doodle?*   *94*

Chapter eleven: *Amazing you!*   *103*

Index   *115*

Introduction

Welcome to the amazing world of graphology! Graphology is the art of reading character from handwriting. Handwriting is a bit like a fingerprint – everybody's is individual, and while two people may write in a very similar fashion, if you look closely you will spot differences. Your handwriting is formed by tiny impulses from your brain. To the trained eye it shows what you are really thinking and feeling – and reveals what an amazing person you are!

In this book you will learn many of the easy-to-spot clues you can get from handwriting. Your friends will be an open book – and you'll learn more about yourself, too.

As soon as you look at a sample of writing you will notice which way the writing slopes, how large it is and where it is placed on the page. When you get a letter you'll have the sender all sussed before you even open it because of the way he or she has written your address. Most people do doodles in class when the teacher is droning on, but these tell you much more about the doodler than that they're getting bored. And did you know the colour you like to write in gives away lots about your personality? Once you're wised up all these things will speak volumes!

When you learn to put all this together you'll have a pretty good idea what makes people tick. You can decide which of your friends it's best to hang out with when you want to have fun and who's the one to have on side when the school bully comes along. You'll understand your folks a bit better and get a real insight into why boys behave the way they do. There are quizzes and games for you to test yourself and even amazing ways of using what you know about graphology to bring out the real you. All you need is some paper, a pen and this book.

So get reading – and get scribbling!

CHAPTER ONE

Secrets of graphology

The science of graphology is based on the knowledge that minute impulses from the brain cause everyone's handwriting to be individual. The theory is that these tiny variations are caused by the fact that everyone thinks differently. Graphologists believe that all the factors in a person's handwriting come from their own special character and brain – sometimes graphology is called 'brainwriting'.

✶⅄ THE HISTORY OF GRAPHOLOGY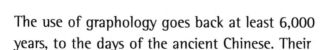

The use of graphology goes back at least 6,000 years, to the days of the ancient Chinese. Their

learning was handed on to the Greeks and
Romans, and the Emperor Nero used it to decide
which people he could trust. Like so much
in the way of knowledge, the science of
graphology was passed down through the
Dark Ages (late 5th century to AD 1000) by
the monks.

The first book to appear on the subject was
written by an Italian, Camillo Baldi, in 1622.
However, the actual word 'graphology' was coined
by Jean Michon, from Paris, in the nineteenth
century. It comes from the Greek word 'graph'
which means writing, and 'ology' which means
study. Michon founded the Graphological Society
in Paris, which flourished until the time of the
Second World War (1939-45). The writer Edgar
Allen Poe also studied handwriting
and published some of his findings,
coining the word 'autography' to
describe his approach.

Graphology was studied at the Harvard
Psychological Clinic in 1930 by Gordon Allport,
and in 1955 Klara Roman and George Staemphli
developed a list of factors that are important in
judging character from handwriting. In many

European universities graphology is part of the curriculum for psychology, but that is not the case everywhere, and some people remain sceptical.

GRAPHOLOGY TODAY

Nowadays there are many areas in life where graphology is deemed extremely useful. Judging handwriting is a great help when assessing people for jobs or in partnership compatibility. Many employers will use a graphologist to analyse a person's writing on their job application, to see whether they are decisive, have leadership qualities, can be relied upon, etc.

Graphology is also used in criminology, forensics and counselling. Handwriting analysis is very important in deciding whether or not a document may be forged; and while this is not quite graphology, as it does not involve interpretation of character, it still relies on the fact that everyone writes differently and that very minute variations can give the game away.

Graphology can also be used by experts to diagnose mental illness, and may be used by the police to gain an insight into the mental health of a suspect.

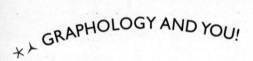
✳✳ GRAPHOLOGY AND YOU!

So how can you use graphology in your everyday life? You can use it to get a better idea about your own character and abilities, and also to get a much deeper understanding of your friends and your family. If you can get a glimpse of a lad's handwriting this can give you a clue as to how good a date he would be and whether you would be suited to each other.

However, graphology, as all skills, needs to be treated with respect. It isn't really fair to pinch a big sample of someone's writing and pull them apart with your friends, without them even  knowing about it! Also, don't talk people into giving you samples of their writing if they don't want to. They have a right to their privacy, and you'll have much more fun with the writing of someone who really wants to take part and who will tell you if you're 'spot on' or not – that way you'll learn even more.

Another thing to remember – don't get too serious! To become really skilled at graphology takes years of study and practice. If you think you see clear signs that someone is mean, or dishonest, just remember that there may be other signs in their writing that they are just the opposite, that you may not have noticed – it's all about weighing things up. Always use your common sense and good judgement, and be careful about jumping to conclusions. What we are covering in this book is very simple and basic – so now let's get on to the fun stuff!

The three zones

In the following pages you will often see the 'zones' mentioned because these are a very important part of graphology. All handwriting is divided into three zones: upper, middle and lower.

graphology

✧ The upper zone is where you find the upper stems and loops of letters like 'b', 'd' and 'h'.

✧ The middle zone is the part just above the line. Letters like small 'a' and 'o' have only a middle zone.

✧ The lower zone is the part where you find the lower strokes of letters like 'g', 'p' and 'y'.

Getting to know these three zones is vital. Soon you will be able to see at a glance whether a person has one of these zones emphasized and that will tell you important things about them.

The upper zone is all about dreams, ideals and even religious or spiritual matters, so a high or well-marked upper zone can indicate someone who isn't very concerned about the day-to-day.

The middle zone is about friendship and everyday life. In many young people this is the biggest zone, because you are interested in being part of a group and learning about life.

The lower zone is about instincts, activities,

energy and motivation. It shows how you feel about money, possessions and the powers of your body. Someone who has a strong lower zone with well-formed loops may be quite athletic. If the loops are very rounded that may also mean imagination, but of a more practical kind than loops in the upper zone.

Writing slant

The way writing slants is another very important indication of a person's character. This refers to the slope of the upstrokes and downstrokes which can be to the right, /; or the opposite way, \, to the left; or straight and vertical.

It is often easy to spot slope. Many people do have a mixture of slopes, but there is usually a general tendency one way or the other.

Although handwriting shows character and is entirely individual, character can and does change as you get older. Your handwriting changes with it. One of the things that often changes is the slope.

✧ Writing that slopes to the right means a
person who is quite outgoing and confident
(although because graphology is complicated,
this isn't the whole story).

meeting people

✧ Writing that stands straight up means a
person who feels able to stand on their own
two feet, who isn't too bothered about what
others think and whose head rules their heart.

independent

✧ Writing that slopes backwards, to the left,
shows a person who is shy and who feels safer
with their own family.

holding back

✧ Writing that has variable slopes means
someone who is changeable and
unpredictable.

Often when you are young your writing slopes slightly backwards because you aren't quite as self-confident as you might like people to think. As you get older and more experienced, your writing may start to slope to the right. Slope of the handwriting comes into play in many areas, so get used to spotting it!

✳⅄ LEFT-HANDERS

Most graphologists believe that being left-handed doesn't affect the slant of the writing or its meanings. Not so long ago people who wrote naturally with their left hand were often made to use their right hand, as it was considered 'odd' to be left-handed! Needless to say, this was very bad for the poor people who were left-handed and some developed a stammer or other sign of nerves as a result. Thank goodness nowadays we have much more sense! However it does mean that there has been less time to study the actual meanings of left-handedness. When you get to know the basics of graphology really well, why not have a really good look at the way your left-handed friends write. Do you think the same rules apply?

✕⅄ MAKING CONNECTIONS

Joined-up writing is something you start learning to do when you are about seven. But later on your writing, and that of your friends, will settle in its own way, and that way might not be very joined at all.

Joined-up script shows a person who thinks logically and in an orderly way, making connections between what they say, do and think. Writing that is hardly joined up at all may mean a loner – someone who is full of ideas and thinks for themselves. If the writing is partly joined, partly disconnected it shows a combination of logic and intuition and can be a sign of creativeness.

all together

individual

Size

In the following chapters we shall often be looking at the size of someone's handwriting. Size of writing may vary a bit, though, depending on how much space is available, so don't be too hasty when judging size, especially of the signature. The signature needs to be compared with the rest of the writing for its size to be accurately interpreted (but more on this in Chapter seven). Big writing can mean a big ego but could equally be someone who mouths off a lot but feels small inside. Small writing means someone who cares about the details.

big   small

Line

Does the writing keep to the line? Or is it dancing just a bit above the line? Maybe it's sloping upwards, or downwards as if trying to get underneath the line. Often the writing won't be on lined paper, so then you need to decide where

an imaginary line would be and make up your
mind from there. The line of the writing is
actually easy to spot when you look at the whole
page and it can give you lots of information
about a person. Generally an upward slope means
optimism while going down ...
well, you've guessed!

it's fab!

Shape of the script

Making up your mind about the 'shape' of the
script takes a longer look but is very simple.
Here's a quick guide:

Cupped writing looks very smooth and relaxed as
it flows across the page. There seem to be lots of
little saucers in this script so even the 'm's look a
bit like 'w's. Here we have a real softie who cares
about everyone.

welcome !

Angular writing is full of sharp corners and angles. In extreme examples even rounded letters, like 'c', can be written as angles. This person could be a bit prickly and very logical.

k ind of prickly !

Arched writing is when there seem to be a lot of archways, as if the script is trying to take off and go upwards. Letters like 'm' and 'n' are well-formed. This person likes to do things the right way! They are probably artistic, too.

making things

Running thread writing is a script that runs almost flat, like a thread, with many of the up and down strokes ironed out. This person likes to manipulate people and doesn't miss a trick! Writing that is not quite so flattened looks more like a wavy line and is less extreme, indicating adaptability.

manipulative!

'Just so' writing is very neat handwriting where all the letters are carefully formed according to some model. Sometimes this may mean the person is hiding something, although with young people it can mean you are just trying hard to get it right!

neat and tidy

Writing speed

Sometimes you can tell how fast someone writes just by looking at their script. Some writing almost leaps off the page while other handwriting is painstaking. However, you may not even need to see the script itself – if you see someone writing you can tell how fast they are moving the pen. You already have some information about them!

Fast writing Fast writers are quick-minded, easily bored and need lots of stimulation. Usually they have lots of get-up-and-go and may rush into things without thinking them through. They are adaptable and extrovert, but they are also able to stand back from situations and weigh them up impartially. However, sometimes they may go off at half cock because they forget to get organized. They may change their minds easily, or be persuaded. Their concentration may lapse, they can be too hasty and you can't always rely on them. There is usually something happening around them, and if there isn't they create it!

Very fast writing This can be a sign of anxiety – it's as if the writer is afraid to slow down in case they are caught out in some way. There is a crazy streak to this person and they may be very tense and impulsive.

Slow writing Here we have a very cautious person who worries a lot (especially about getting things right). Their mind works slowly and they may be painfully self-conscious. They tend to believe anything you tell them but they are very careful about committing themselves. They can be couch potatoes, full of reasons not to do things.

15

However, they are neat, reliable and steady.
What you see is what you get, and you'll
get the same tomorrow, and the next day,
and the next ...

Writing at normal speed This shows balance,
relaxation and fluency. There is no wish to dawdle
but the writer is not prepared to sacrifice quality
and clarity for speed. They will tend to have this
attitude to life in general.

Over to you

Those are some of the basics of the science of
graphology. Have you absorbed most of them?
Why not try this quick quiz to see how many of
the answers you have at your fingertips?

Quick quiz – the basics

1) Which of the three zones might be the most noticeable in a girl who was always dreaming, writing poetry and sending off letters to her MP about cruelty to animals?

2) What might it mean if your writing slopes backwards, to the left?

3) If you like all your writing to be joined up, what does this say about you?

4) If your writing is very big, does that definitely mean you are very confident?

5) If your friend is great at cheering you up and always has a big grin on her face, would you expect the line of her writing to be going upwards, towards the right, or downwards?

6) If you want someone who's really easy to be with and listens to you, which basic writing shape would be your best bet?

7) What does fast writing reveal about someone?

8) Could you expect someone with slow writing to always be the centre of attention?

All the answers are easy to get from the chapter. Count up your score – no cheating!

0-2 correct Well, you've got a lot to learn, but you obviously realize that this is a complicated subject. And at least you're honest with yourself, so that's a good basis to get better. Why not go over the chapter again and remind yourself of the basics.

 3-5 correct Not a bad start – keep going!

 6-8 correct Fantastic! Congratulations!

Whatever your score, there's lots more to learn, so read on!

CHAPTER TWO

Pen pals

A knowing look at your friend's scrawl will tell you more than whether she's good at spelling! Check out her writing to see how great a mate she is.

✶⅄ FUN TO BE WITH?

If her writing slopes to the right then chances are she likes to be with the crowd. If her writing is very wide, she likes to be the centre of attention. If you want to get up to something daring, she's your girl – only watch that she doesn't go over the top! If you want a real live-wire look out for

Look at me!

writing that rises upwards from the line – she's got attitude, energy and she'll have a go at anything. Can you keep up? If she leaves no margins at the right of her script, she grabs life with both hands and doesn't worry about the future.

If her writing slopes to the left she'll probably rather have you round at hers than go out, because she feels safer at home. If there are great big spaces between her words, chances are she feels lonely inside, but it could be hard to get her to talk about it. If her writing is very narrow she's insecure – why not give her some TLC? If her writing tends to slope downwards, she could be a bit gloomy. You may have to put some effort into cheering her up!

I'm a bit shy!

✷⅄ CAN YOU TRUST HER?

Trust is very important in a friend. You'll need more than a look at her handwriting to be sure, but it can give you a good indication. If she's got the signs of being good fun, then it's likely that the first thing on her mind isn't watching what she says! If she draws her little 'x' in two parts, like two semi-circles – ꭉ – then she's a motormouth. If her little 'o's are open at the top, then she spills the beans all over the place, and if her 'a's are the same – ꭒ ꭎ – watch out! She's the first with the gossip and if you take her into your confidence about something juicy she just might not be able to resist passing it on. But of course, all of that means she's open – at least you know where you are with her!

Be more careful if her little 'o's and 'a's are open at the bottom – *open* – because then she might deceive you. If her 'a's and 'o's are rolled round – *open* – then she can keep a secret, and probably has a few up her sleeve.

If you just want a friend who's reliable, sensible and well-balanced, look for writing that is well set-out, with average and equal distances between the words. You'll know she's dependable and down-to-earth.

✦↙ WILL SHE LEND YOU HER GEAR?

It's great to have a friend who'll let you borrow your best stuff. What are the signs that she'll let you rummage in her cupboard – or keep it firmly closed?

If her writing is very narrow, chances are she'll be hanging on to everything for dear life! She doesn't want to be mean – she just worries about everything, and however much she likes you she just can't seem to trust you with her best things.

I'm a bit shy!

Look at me!

Wider writing means she's likely to be generous. If her script is very wide, you can bet that she doesn't know where half her stuff is, anyway! If her capital 'A' has a horizontal stroke that looks like a cup – Ậ – then she's easygoing. If the upper loops on her capital 'P's and 'R's are large – P R – then she's likely to want to look after you – lucky you!

22

★ WHAT'S SHE LIKE WHEN THAT BULLY COMES ALONG?

We all know that the best way to deal with bullies is to tell a responsible adult about them, so that the problem can be dealt with. But if you're being bullied and there's no older person in sight, the last thing you want is a friend who'll run off and leave you. So check out your friend's handwriting to be sure she'll stick up for you.

Look out for a capital 'T' where the top bar extends over the word – this means that this girl is protective, although she might talk down to you at times. She's not likely to leave you high and dry and may stick up for you where she wouldn't for herself.

Check out the pressure of her writing. The way to do that is to run your fingers under her page. Can you feel the little dents? Then she pushes hard! This could mean she's stubborn and snarly a lot of the time, but when her back's up against the wall, she's probably fearless. She's got

23

a will of iron and bags of energy. The only
drawback is she could end up losing her rag.

If the pressure of her writing is very light
that's harder to spot than heavy pressure but if
you look closely you might see that some
of the strokes are hardly visible, because the
pen has been almost floating over the page!
She's probably not very energetic and tends to
give way if pushed. Her will isn't that strong,
but she's a sensitive soul and may be very
understanding. She could be light on her feet
and have eyes in the back of her head – which
could certainly come in handy! If her writing is
very narrow, especially the 'm' and 'n', then she
may be timid and not very confident.

IS SHE THE TEACHER'S PET?

Teacher's pet isn't so bad! Chances are she's
a clever clogs and can help you with your
homework when you need a helping hand. Look
out for generally neat and evenly set-out work –
just the sort of tidy stuff you'd expect.

If her capital letters have flourishes, then she's a show-off. She wants everyone to think she's special – including the teacher. If the second arch on her capital 'M' is higher than the first – *m* – then she's dying to get that star. A little 'y' that has a tail going straight down – *y* – tells you her concentration is good. A capital 'O' with a curling upper loop that looks as if it's trying to take off – *O* – means she thinks on her feet. If all of her upper zone is very tall, then she's always aiming high, and it's not just in the classroom she wants to do well – she's idealistic about life, too. Someone like that can be great to be with, because she'll make you think about your own values and what's important to you in life.

If her little 'k' or 'r' is written like a capital, then she's got attitude and she's more into being 'her' than fitting in with other people's expectations. If the upper part of her 'k' forms a loop then she's a rebel. If her writing's very large, then she believes the teacher should think she's great without her trying very hard.

★ ✳ ★ ★

25

✶✓ WHAT'S SHE LIKE WITH THE LADS?

A girl who loves to hang around with the lads is great if that's what you enjoy doing too! If she writes her 'c' like a filled-in crescent moon – 𝐜 – colours in the bottom of her 'f' – 𝐟 – and the top of her 'e' – 𝐞 – then she's got boys on her mind. If her lower zone is strong, with deep,

yes, dreamy

well-formed loops, she can't wait to cuddle up next to the boy of her dreams. If those underloops are wide and open, like cups, then she's a hopeless romantic. If those loops are very large, and if the stroke comes up and cuts through the middle zone, then the boys better watch out! She'll need you to help keep her mind on other things.

yes dreamy

JJamlet

If her capital letters are very fussy, then she wants to grab all the attention from the lads and she could be quite vain. Check out the dot over her small 'i' – is it written like a small circle? Then she's a drama queen! If her capital

'N' starts with a small curl – η – then she could be jealous of you. A capital 'M' that has a little loop on its left upright – $\mathcal{M}$ – means the same thing – so watch out!

If her script is generally rounded, with the middle zone emphasized then she's *Sweetie* a sweetie who wants the lads to love her. If there are large loops at the top of her letters then she's likely to be a dreamer. Her mind *high hopes* could be on her favourite pop star rather than the boy next door.

Does her writing look very angular? Her head probably rules her heart. She won't *critical* get carried away and she could be a bit critical of your crush. Very narrow letters mean she keeps her feelings well-hidden – not much fun for girlie chats but at least she won't go over-the-top.

★ DOES SHE WANT TO GET CLOSE?

If her writing is generally well-rounded, with a large middle zone, then she loves her friends as well as the guys. She's probably practical –

27

fantastic when it comes to organizing
sleepovers – but she may make a bit of
a fuss over nothing and she could be
selfish. If her writing slopes to the right then she's
a 'people person'. She's not happy on her own for
long and she wants to give to others and
communicate. If she writes her words very close

stay with me together then she just can't cope
with being alone – she needs to
be with a gang, and although it might seem like
she wants closeness it may be hard to get her
away from the crowd. Very curved writing with
big, rounded capitals means she's emotional,
wears her heart on her sleeve and has a good blub
every now and then. A capital 'E' written like two
semi-circles – ξ – shows she's warm-hearted and a
big top loop to her capital 'R' tells you she's kind.

If her writing slopes to the left then it'll take
longer to get to know her and it'll be a while
before she trusts you. If the spaces between her
words are very wide, she's afraid to get close, but
this might change as she gets older. Narrow
capitals mean she's shy – give her a chance to
come out of her shell.

Over to you

This chapter has given you an idea of how to recognize the writing of the type of friend you may want. Always remember, though, not to make judgements that are too hard and fast. Just because you haven't spotted a sign of something in a person's handwriting, doesn't mean it isn't there!

If you haven't already done this, find a large sample of your own writing, preferably one you did before knowing anything about graphology. What does it tell you? Are you surprised?

Now think about two or three of your best friends. Get a pen and some paper and make a note of at least six things you would say about them. Write what comes to mind first.

As soon as you can, try to get a sample of writing from each of your friends – make sure you

ask them first! Does it match what you thought? What can you spot that's the same? Or different? If the writing tells you things that surprise you, could it be

that you've only seen part of her personality?
Ask your friend what she thinks about your
findings. As always, have fun and don't take
this too seriously. The best way to really get to
know someone is to spend time with them.
Graphology can help give you useful pointers
but it's not the full story.

CHAPTER THREE

Love letters

If you've got a crush on a lad then you think he's Mr Wonderful. When we really like someone it's easy to be blind to their faults. We sometimes even see them as completely different from how they actually are. Take a peek at your crush's writing to see if your impressions are correct!

✳⅄ ENERGETIC AND SPORTY

Does he try to impress you with his trendy trainers and sporty clothes? You won't need to watch him play footie to know how sporty he really is. Take a look at the lower zone of his writing.

Sporty

If his downstrokes are long and firm, he's energetic, and if his lower loops are well-formed then it's even more certain. Do the touchy-feely test at the back of the paper to see if his pressure is hard. This means he's a force to be reckoned with and is probably quite scary on the rugby pitch! If his writing tries to go below the line when there's no need, such as with the final downstroke of 'm', then he's very physical indeed.

It's no surprise that writing that's spidery and feeble tends to show a guy who uses mind rather than muscle. If his script is narrow then he's probably too worried about getting hurt to play hero – but you never know!

✗λ IS HE ROMANTIC?

If his middle zone is rounded and his lower loops *romantic boy* are well-formed and open then he's a Romeo. If there are big round loops on the top of his 'h's, 'k's and 'l's then be gentle with him – he's very sensitive and emotional – *kiss him*. If his capital 'B' has a large lower loop then he'll believe anything – so don't show him up in front of his mates! *Believe!*

If his middle zone is very small then he could be quite cool and detached. Team that with a high upper zone and his mind's on higher things. Unless you share his *higher matters* ideals he might not be very interesting to be with.

cool and controlled Angular writing tells you he's not a very warm person, although you can probably rely on him.

✕⅄ TAKE NOTE OF HIS NOTE

If a lad sends you a note, be careful how you assess it. Boys are generally less careful about the way they write. A scruffy note may mean he wants to look 'cool', not that he doesn't care. But if he's obviously taken great trouble with his writing, then he wants to impress you – it isn't rocket science!

Look out for little indications such as words that he's written in an extra-wobbly way, or formed carefully – this may be a sign of strong emotion. For instance, has he written your name differently from the rest of his writing? Do some words look cramped, or rushed, as if he's embarrassed? If he's finished off with 'love from' how has he written the word 'love'? If you don't trust yourself to decide, ask a good friend what she thinks!

The meanings of margins

If a lad sends you a note then you hold a lot of information about him in your hand. The first things to look at are the margins he leaves around his writing.

Top margin If he leaves a lot of space at the top of the page, before he even starts to write, then he's hesitating. He might want you to make the first move – he's not very confident. He could also be extravagant and used to a life of luxury. If his top margin is very small then he could be careful with money. Don't expect him to buy you a coke and pizza!

Bottom margin A lot of space at the bottom of his page could mean he's only written a short note. But if he goes on to another page and leaves space for another few lines then he's afraid of emotion and getting involved. If he goes right on to the bottom of the page, the opposite is likely, so watch out! This guy likes to jump in with both feet. He could also be a bit over-concerned with money and all it can buy.

Right-hand margin Lots of space at the right of his page means he worries a lot. He could have some specific problem or be afraid of what the future holds. He probably needs a listening ear, but it wouldn't be a good idea to push him to talk because that would worry him too. If he writes up to the edge of the page then he's a go-getter with lots of energy. He probably gets into scrapes because he doesn't know the meaning of 'look before you leap', but he's confident enough to get himself out of them. He's a great communicator, but doesn't believe all he hears! Right-hand margins are bound to go in and out a bit because not all words are the same length, but if his varies more than it has to then he's got more of a sense of adventure than others and he could be unpredictable.

Left-hand margin Loads of space at the left of the page could show he's very well brought-up (and he knows it!). He likes the good life but isn't that much of a party animal – unless it's at The Ritz! Hardly any space at the left means he could have a really big mouth and always be putting his foot in it, but he wants people to like him. Chances are he's a bit low on cash, or maybe he just wants to hang on to it! If the left-hand margin goes in and out a bit, or slopes, then it means he's changeable. The amount of space at the top of the page shows how he'll start out, but he might not keep to it.

Big margin all round If his writing looks like it's in the middle of the page with a large 'frame' of emptiness around it, then he feels lonely and misunderstood. He's secretive and afraid – he thinks he's safer by himself and builds an invisible wall around himself.

No margins at all He's turned 'waste not, want not' into an obsession, so don't expect him to lend you your bus fare!

Over to you

Have you got any old letters lying around? Remember that all of the previous interpretations can also be used on the letters of your relatives and friends, if they write you a note. The longer the letter, the more you have to go on. It's not always what you write but the way it looks on the page!

Quick quiz – margin matters

Try this quiz to see if you can
remember what's what with margins.

What does it mean if someone leaves:

1) a big top margin?

2) a big bottom margin?

3) a big right-hand margin?

4) a big left-hand margin?

5) a big margin all round?

6) no margin at all?

Check your answers in the chapter. How did you
do? Hopefully you've surprised yourself by how
much you've picked up – you're well on your way
to becoming a great graphologist!

CHAPTER FOUR

Family ABC

Sometimes family members will have similar writing. If you admire your Mum, Dad, foster parents or guardians you may want to write the way they do. If you want to rebel you might like to write in a very different way. Your attitude to your family will show in the way you write your name.

⋆⅄ FAMILY PRIDE

If you write your surname much larger than your first name, you are very proud of where you come from. However, it could be dwarfing your individuality. The same applies if you start your surname with a very big capital. If your Mum has

taken your Dad's name, take a look at her
signature to see how happy she is about this!
If her surname looks cramped compared to her
first name, maybe she feels her own independence
is important.

 Sense of individuality This will be shown if the
pressure and emphasis on the first name is
stronger than on the surname. You are your own
person, not a 'chip off the old block'. You may
wish your family would notice you for who
you are.

 Hiding away If you tend to write your first
names just as initials, where you can, then maybe
you are trying to hide your true self behind your
family; or perhaps you feel your family
overshadows you in some way.

⋆⅄ KEEPING TIDY

One of the major issues round the house is
probably keeping your stuff sorted and your room
in order. A look at your writing will show whether

you are naturally neat and tidy. A glance at Mum's writing might let you know just how tidy she really is, when left to her own devices!

Script that is even and well-spaced out, easy to read, with the 'i's neatly dotted and the 't's crossed indicates a tidy mind. If the words and letters are consistently formed and there is an overall 'rhythm' to the writing, then the writer has plenty of self-control and sense of the proper way to do things. If you write like this you are probably pretty organized even if you haven't brought this to bear on that battle-zone of a room!

On the other hand, writing that is disjointed, scrawling and generally all over the place not surprisingly hints at someone who tends to lead a chaotic life. If there is no dot at all over the 'i' this means carelessness and absentmindedness – this writer will be doing well if they manage to wear matching socks! If the dot on the 'i' is variable, sometimes there, sometimes not, sometimes ahead of the 'i', sometimes behind it, then the writer believes that variety is the spice of life and that tidiness is generally boring.

However, they may have a blitz every so often, just for the hell of it! If the dot is to the left of the 'i' the writer means to be tidy but never quite gets round to it – until they run out of excuses!

MONEY MATTERS

Getting your folks to increase your allowance is probably on your mind quite a lot. Checking out their handwriting will help give you a clue as to how they feel about money matters.

If your Mum or Dad writes their capital 'A' with the left vertical stroke like a loop – A – then they have money on their minds, liking to know exactly where it's going, and whether they are getting value for it, etc. This won't mean they necessarily say 'no', but they may like to have something to show for it. Offering to wash the car or do the ironing could convince them it's worth it!

If the writing shows lots of tiny 'hooks' at the end of letters, getting money could be more of a challenge – this person just doesn't want to part with their cash! Signs to look out for are a capital 'C' with a stroke at the base going back to the left – $\mathcal{C}$. The same goes for capital 'P', small 'j' and small 'q' – q j – all these letters may show a very small curved stroke that 'claws back' indicating the writer likes to keep valuables to him or her self. This is probably because they felt deprived at some time in the past. Don't make too many demands.

If there are signs in the writing that look like '£' or '$' this shows an aptitude for money and an interest in the whole subject. The person may be very good at making money and may part with it if you show that you, too, understand its value. Signs to look for are a capital 'I' or 'L' that look like a pound or dollar sign – $\mathcal{L}$. Aptitude for finances is also hinted at by a small 'l' that looks like a '0' – ℓ.

If the writing, in general, is very narrow and cramped then getting more money will be like getting blood out of a stone! However, if the writing is wide, this is a much better sign. If the capital 'H' is wider than it is high – $\vdash\dashv$ – we have the last of the big spenders so make sure you're close by when the purse comes out!

✶⅄ BEING BOSS

Who's boss in your family?
Handwriting can give you major clues.

A very long bar across a 't' shows protective
instincts, good management and the ability to

taking care

see the 'big picture'. This person will
naturally take on a leadership role
but they will have the imagination

to appreciate how to get the best out of people
without bossing – for the most part! If the 't' bar
is to the right of the 't' and
sweeping upwards, this person
is going to get their own way!

taking care

If the dot of the 'i' is close to the top of the
upright stroke then this writer makes their
presence felt and can be very demanding and
particular. No getting away without doing your
homework when this parent or guardian is on
your case!

A capital 'F' or capital 'T' with the horizontal
stroke extending far to the right shows a
protective but rather superior attitude. This person
knows just how to make you feel small.

Small 'm' with the final downstroke plunging below the line – *m̦ind!* – could mean temper tantrums – so keep out of the way!

If the capitals are generally pretty big but not overly large, the writer likes to be respected and listened to. If you argue with them they could take it personally, especially if you are in the right. Your best bet is to make sure you're in their good books. If the capitals are very large, watch out! This person might act like royalty but doesn't feel secure so they could be a bit touchy and condescending.

⋆⋋ KEEPING THE PEACE

Every family should have a peacemaker. Can you spot yours?

Lots of 'saucers' in writing Look at a writing sample that is reasonably long. Do the joins between the letters look like shallow dishes, as if the writing is one long garland?

In Chapter one we looked at writing like this (see page 12). It usually means a very peace-loving and gentle person who can see everybody's point of view. They will avoid arguments because they see no point in them, and they will adapt to the other person's wishes in most cases. Kind, warm-hearted and accepting, this person is not weak, just accommodating. They are sympathetic to all, and their sincerity means they have the ability to make people see what they have in common. Their relaxed attitude means they are great in most situations, but they can get depressed if there is a lot of strife.

Capital 'H' where the horizontal bar rises from the upright and juts out to the right – This writer knows how to get out of scrapes and will generally have a quick answer or clever excuse. Look out also for writing that flattens out into a thread. Here is an opportunist who can manipulate people and think on their feet. If your brother or sister has thread-like writing, watch out that you aren't the one left to carry the can! The 'peace' that this writer keeps is usually to their own advantage.

Rounded capitals and small 'p's These show a kind and gentle nature. Rounded 'c's and 's's have a similar meaning. *Very sweet*

★ SENSE OF HUMOUR

A good laugh is a life-saver when things are getting fraught. What are the signs to spot the comedian of the family?

Starting strokes Some people make small strokes at the start of their letters. Look out for strokes like a small scoop or wave – *boo!* – these show a sense of humour. But beware if the starting stroke is a hook – *boo!*. This person may be aggressive and doesn't give up when they want something.

An 'i' dot that looks like a comma – i This shows a wicked wit and a talent for sarcasm. This person may poke fun at you – take it in good part!

47

Through the ages

Everybody's writing changes with age, although it
is rarely possible to tell a person's age from their
writing, unless they are very old (when their
writing is likely to be wavering) or very young
(when it will be carefully and crudely formed).
As you go through life your personality alters.
You may become more confident, or less so; you
may care more about what your friends think or
you may become more independent. There are
so many ways that you can change.

In times gone by, people were encouraged –
even compelled – to write a certain way. Writing
usually sloped to the right, because it looks more
'flowing', and there was a correct way to form
each letter. Of course a trained graphologist could
still spot character traits, for if you have
been forced to write in a way that
doesn't suit you, the tension shows in
small ways in your writing.

Nowadays, of course, there is much more
freedom. At some point in junior school you start
to do joined-up writing, but many people choose

48

to carry on printing their letters and eventually develop their own style. By the time you have reached 25 or 30 it is quite possible that your writing will be totally different from the way it is now! It is fascinating to see how writing changes over a lifetime and to see that the way a person has developed has really been 'spelled out'.

Over to you

Get a sample of your writing from a year ago, from two years ago, or even three or more. Compare it closely with the way you write now. What are the differences? Here are some things you might spot:

Slant Has the slant changed? Is your writing sloping more to the right, showing you're more interested in relationships; or more to the left, showing you're more 'into' yourself?

Round middle zone Has your middle zone become less round, showing you're developing interests that have little to do with being liked by your friends; or more rounded, showing you're even more sociable?

Dotting 'i's and crossing 't's Are you doing these things more or less regularly and neatly? If it is the former then you're becoming more organized, tidy and generally sorted. If not, then it's the opposite!

Bigger or smaller When you are young you often write quite large letters partly because it is easier (when you're very small, at least), but also because you don't have much confidence so you write big to make up for it. If your writing has got bigger this could be because you feel more assured, or if it is really large it's more likely that you're trying to make up for not feeling so good inside. Smaller writing may mean you're shyer now than you used to be. It could also mean you've got things more into proportion now you're older.

Joined up or separate If all your letters are separate this doesn't mean you're 'young for your age'. It is more likely to mean that you stand on your own two feet, that you have your own 'take' on things, and also that you are creative and artistic. If some letters are joined while others are separate, this shows flashes of intuition. If all your letters are joined, you are probably very logical and calm.

These are just a few of the ways your writing can change over time. Look closely at your samples and thumb through this book to spot the meanings. You could find you've changed more than you realize!

CHAPTER FIVE

Your talents in your writing

It can be quite hard to be sure what you're good at, or even what you'd like to do in life. Your family may have expectations which you feel you should live up to – or rebel against. The things you are good at, at school, might not seem to lead to attractive careers. Maybe a glance at your writing will give you some pointers.

EXTROVERT/INTROVERT

In the first chapter we looked at the slant of the writing. If your writing slopes to the right then you probably are an extrovert. If it slopes to the left you are more introverted, and if it is upright you are balanced between the two, and are likely to be quite independent.

Writing that slants to the right indicates working with people. If this is you there is no way you would be happy doing lots of things on your own. You need to chat, to exchange ideas and to be friendly. You understand people's feelings and embrace them. You like to have a goal to aim for and you are enthusiastic and versatile. You feel good when you are giving to others, although you are capable of acting on your own initiative and you have original ideas. Careers need to be looked at closely for the amount of company they will offer you. For instance, working in an office with a great bunch of people might be fine, but being in a corner on your own – oh no! The sort of careers that may appeal include social work, counselling, selling and a wide variety of people-centred jobs.

If your writing has a very strong right slant – *impulsive* – then other people have a very great influence on you. You probably give in to them a bit too much, but you can also be very impulsive and impatient. Your feelings are very strong. This means that whatever you do you need to choose your companions with great care because they will have a powerful effect on you. As time goes by, you may find that your writing becomes more vertical as you gain more self-confidence.

Upright writing shows reliability and a cool head. People with this style of writing are realistic, sceptical and able to work alone. Impartiality, independence and the ability to weigh up the written and spoken word suggest careers such as the law, administrative work, management and similar. Any job that calls for initiative and tenacity would be suitable. Because these people are objective and impartial, any job that requires sympathy and a responsive nature would not be first choice. They are better as leaders and organizers where their natural confidence and desire for order can be expressed.

Writing that slopes to the left often shows an introverted person. If this is you, your memory is probably good and you are quietly ambitious and determined to get what you want. You can work on your own if necessary and you always want to improve yourself. You would be best suited to a career that mainly involves working independently. This could be of any sort that gives you the opportunity to develop your skills and meet your own high standards. You have no need to try to force yourself into a more outgoing mode just because everyone seems to prize extroversion – it is fine to be quieter and you will get more done!

Very extreme backward-slanting writing can mean you are quite withdrawn – *withdrawn* – and that your family has a very powerful influence on you and your life. It is hard for you to forget what happened to you in the past and you may feel uncomfortable with your emotions. In time, your writing may become slightly more upright as you learn to relax and accept yourself. Then you'll be able to make the right choice for you.

✕⅄ GOOD WITH FIGURES?

Are you thinking about a career in banking, accountancy or similar? Look out for signs of figures in your writing. A 'B' that looks like '13' shows growing awareness of maths; an 'O' that looks like a perfect zero is similar; also a 'b' that is like '6' – **6** ; and a small 'o' that is also like a zero. Team that with upright or backward-slanting writing and it is likely that numbers may be easier to cope with than people! A neat and even script, especially one that has points rather than loops (i.e. angular), increases the sense of logic and planning ability. What more do you need?

✕⅄ ARTISTIC?

Writing that generally looks like a series of arches denotes an artistic person. Look out also for flowing capitals, especially 'F' – *f* – which show a sensitive and creative temperament. An 'r' which looks like 'c' and letters that look 'painted' – i.e. separate from the rest of the script – all indicate artistic skill and approach.

★⅄ MUSICAL?

Some of the signs of the musical person are similar to that of the artist – for instance, the writing has lots of arches. Look out especially for *music* 'm's and 'n's that have high arches and for letters written like musical notes, such as 'b', 'd' and 'q' – *d q*. Even the capital 'Q' can be written as a large 'q' showing the writer wants to get that musical sign in somewhere!

★⅄ LITERARY?

Maybe you would like to be a writer, editor, publisher or journalist? Creative writers may have writing that seems to be trying to jump off the page. The 't' strokes may be long and link up with the following script, showing the ability to make connections between different ideas. Printed letters, such as capital 'B' and 'F', show the writer is good at English, and shares some characteristics with the painted letters of the artistic person. A 'G' that is like an '8' – δ – shows an aptitude for literature. If you are interested in creative writing, what you write is more important than how you write, so just get busy!

✕⅄ SPORTY?

Hard pressure when you write and long, well-formed loops under letters like 'g' and 'y' are a great indication of physical strength and energy. Upright writing shows persistence – combine the two in a training programme to be a winner.

⋆⋋ PRACTICAL?

Generally a square, careful hand shows a pragmatic nature. A capital 'A' that is formed in square fashion with a horizontal bar where the point would normally be – ⊓ – shows the sort of constructive skill that a builder or engineer might need. The same goes for 'B' written as two boxes, 'a' written as a box with a tail, 'r' written as a right angle and 'c's and 'n's – ɑ ⊏ ⊓ – like three sides of a rectangle. Such shaping shows a good grasp of the material world and what makes things work.

Over to you

In this chapter we've covered quite a few possible talents. If the one you're interested in isn't there, think about what it really involves and decide what comes close. For instance, to be a vet you'd need good people skills and probably a head for figures to get your qualifications as they would involve some maths. To be a model could require some of the stamina of the sporty type – so just use your imagination.

Take a sample of your own handwriting and have a good, long look at it, taking into account all the points made in the chapter. What talents do you have? Do you agree with what your writing reveals, or do you see yourself differently? If so, ask a friend that you trust for her opinion.

If you wish you had a talent that doesn't show, remember two things. Firstly, just because you cannot find something in your writing, doesn't mean it isn't there – not everything is shown in handwriting. Secondly, as time goes by your writing will probably change, and so you may show the development of the talent you desire. But the chances are you'll find out something fabulous about yourself anyway – graphology isn't there to limit you, but to help you discover more.

CHAPTER SIX

Putting on the style

Do you feel sure of your style? Or do you change your mind about what image you like best? As you get older it's fine to alter the way you look, and the different things you feel comfortable with will probably be reflected in your handwriting. For now, check your script for some tell-tale signs. If your writing slants backwards and forwards on the same line, then you change your mind a lot and may have several different styles with which you are happy.

★人 MISS SPORTY

Are there long, strong strokes in your lower zone, with well-formed loops? This shows you have lots of physical energy. This will be even more so if you write with hard pressure, and have angular handwriting with lots of sharp edges. You are happiest in tracksuits, T-shirts and your favourite trendy trainers. Clothes that constrict you or stop you moving freely make you feel frustrated and edgy. Choose loose clothes or ones made from stretch fabrics in bright colours, or black, white or navy, so you look crisp. If you need to look a bit smarter a short denim skirt and hoody should do the trick.

✗⅄ TRAFFIC-STOPPER

Is your writing generally large, with lots of flourishes? Are your capital letters particularly noticeable? Are there loops in your capital 'A's and does the bottom stroke of your capital 'E' or the bottom stroke of little 'c' extend to underline the following word? Do you have great big round capital 'O's? Any or all of these signs can mean you like to be noticed! Wear the

62

latest fashions in glittery fabrics and bright clothes, and make sure that your hairstyle is always extra-special.

✳⅄ PRINCESS

Does your writing seem to have lots of saucer-shaped strokes so it looks a bit like a long garland, as described in Chapter one (see page 12)? Does it slope gently to the right? Are your capitals in proportion and your middle zone generally well-rounded? Then you are probably gentle and feminine and a girly-girly look is just 'you'. Wear floral prints and pastel colours like pink and baby blue. Have your hair long and/or curly and spend time dressing it in a feminine way, with flowery clips or slides. Pretty jewellery is a must, and a bit of lace here and there, on your socks or hemline, will suit your personality.

✶⅄ SMART AND NEAT

Neat writing, with properly dotted 'i's and crossed 't's may well mean that you like to be dressed that way. Look out also for a very slight slope to the right, script that is on the small side, even pressure and form, and equal spacing between the words and lines. If this is you then you probably like your appearance to be neat. Choose your wardrobe carefully to make sure everything is co-ordinated. Check everything for loose buttons and hanging threads and give yourself five minutes each morning to check yourself from head to toe, so you look sharp and ready for anything.

✶⅄ ROMANTIC

Do you have 'tall' writing with loops in the upper zone? Does your 't' bar take off – ⌐ ? Do you write with light pressure? Does the loop of your capital 'D' curve round – 𝒪 – so it cuts through the top of the loop and 'flies away'? Is there a big top loop to your 'G' – G – or a bulbous lower loop to your 'j' and 'g'? Is there a loop to your little 'r' – $ρ$? The more of these signs you have in your writing the more of a dreamer and romantic you are likely to be. Play this up with floaty fabrics, velvet, satin and lace, hoop earrings and long or wavy hairstyles. Take every chance you can to dress up.

✗⅄ INDIVIDUAL

Do you have upright writing with wide spaces between your words? Does your writing look like a series of archways as described in the first chapter? Does your capital 'K' look like a capital 'R' – R ? Does your small 'k' tend to look like a capital or your small 'r' very large? All of these indicate that you are independent and don't always want to look like the rest of the crowd. You've got strength of character and your very own exclusive style. You may find you're able to choose clothes best when you shop alone or with just one friend. Fashionable things may not always appeal – go for unusual styles, interesting accessories, and make sure you customize your gear whenever you can, to make sure that it really is unique.

Over to you

Found your style? Hopefully this chapter will give you a better idea of how to express yourself. Valuing and accepting yourself is a way to radiate confidence. So, are there changes you'd like to make to be more 'you'? Go for it! Just as your handwriting is individual – everyone's style is different. Be yourself and make up your own mind about how you want to look and what you want to wear. Find a style you feel happy and comfortable with and don't be tempted to follow the crowd. Be true to yourself and you'll discover just how amazing you are!

CHAPTER SEVEN

How confident are you?

The way you write your capital 'I' says a lot about your self-esteem and the way you feel about yourself. It will also tell you a lot about the true self-image of your friends – whether they see themselves as a true star or whether they're happier blending in with the crowd.

☆ **Very large capital 'I'**
If the 'I' is very large in comparison with the rest of the script you might assume this means someone who thinks they're wonderful, but actually the opposite is the case. This person is compensating for a very poor self-image by writing this way. Inside they lack confidence and although they may boast and draw attention to themselves, it's just a front.

I mpressive!

☆ **Tiny capital 'I'**
This shows someone who is scared of life and
feels it's safer not to be noticed!

I forgot

☆ **Capital 'I' written as small 'i'**
This person has a very low opinion of themselves.
They need to work on their self-esteem.

i forgot

☆ **Rounded capital 'I'**
If the 'I' is written more like a small 'l' with a
loop, then the writer feels they need to protect
themselves in some way.

l forgot

☆ **Balanced capital 'I'**
A plain, simple, upright stroke shows healthy
self-esteem and a clear mind. This person is happy
to be what they are and feels no need to impress.
They probably have good judgement in most
matters.

I am sure

☆ **Big, curvy 'I'**
This person tends to go over-the-top. They may be too big for their boots.

☆ **'I' with horizontal strokes**
If the 'I' is written in this printed fashion then the writer is probably good at English, loves reading and may even write their own stories or poetry.

☆ **'I' written like '9' or '1'**
An aptitude for figures is shown here, or someone who thinks about money a lot of the time. As we saw earlier (see page 43), an 'I' written like a '£' or '$' sign is another indication of money-mindedness.

☆ **Very narrow capital 'I'**
This will usually be found in writing that is also narrow. It means the writer's natural desires and ability to enjoy life are restricted. If the 'I' looks even narrower than the rest of the script this will be even more marked. This writer needs to learn how to relax and truly enjoy life.

☆ **Sharp capital 'I'**
Anger is indicated by an 'I' that looks like a
weapon. Healthy outlets need to be found for
aggression, such as taking up a new
sport or going for a nice long walk.

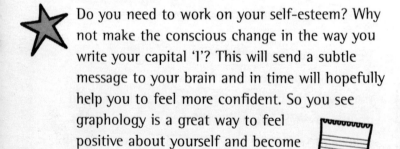

☆ **An 'I' that slopes in a different direction from
the rest of the script**
This indicates that the writer feels
they do not fit in. For some reason they are not
at ease – possibly they feel they have done
something wrong. If the 'I' slopes backwards to
the left then they probably wish to draw back.
If it slopes the other way then they feel they
have to make up to someone for something.

Do you need to work on your self-esteem? Why
not make the conscious change in the way you
write your capital 'I'? This will send a subtle
message to your brain and in time will hopefully
help you to feel more confident. So you see
graphology is a great way to feel
positive about yourself and become
more in touch with the real you.

Sign it! What your signature reveals

The most 'conscious' type of writing is when we sign our names. We are aware that we may be giving an impression of ourselves. Young people often try to develop a 'grown up' signature – and we like our signature to be special. The good thing about signatures is they are easy to spot, and even if you have no other clues – for instance, in a typewritten letter – the signature will be there. However, while a signature can tell you a lot about a person, it really needs to be compared with the rest of the script to see what sort of an overall 'image' the person likes to create.

✧ **Signature just like the rest of the writing**
What you see is what you get! This person is natural, has no 'side' and doesn't try to appear to be what she or he isn't.

✧ **Large signature**

A large signature is most significant when compared with the rest of the script. It shows a wish to be noticed and to be listened to, but it doesn't necessarily mean the person is confident.

Signature

In fact they may well lack assurance and try to make up for this by writing their name so it can't be missed. Film stars and pop idols often have big signatures, or ones that really stand out because they need to project that larger-than-life impression. Inside they may feel very different. Someone who writes their name very large doesn't always have a big ego – they may just be naturally outgoing and confident. If a signature seems to expand outside the space allowed for it, for instance on a document or cheque, then this person probably feels rules are made to be broken and likes to push boundaries to the limit.

✧ **Small signature**

Generally this indicates someone who is quite happy to blend in with the crowd and not draw attention to themselves. A signature that is made smaller to fit the space available may show someone who is very aware of their surroundings and social space – the writer likes to 'fit in'. Just because someone has a small signature, doesn't mean they are 'small' in any way. Successful people can have small signatures if they prefer privacy and seclusion.

Signature

✧ **On the dotted line**

Usually when we sign our name it is pretty obvious where we should put it. Even when writing a casual note the 'natural' position for the signature can be seen. If a signature is placed in a balanced way, in the centre of the available space, then the writer probably has both self-esteem and respect for others. If the name is to the left, this person may be rather timid, if it is to the right they are probably scatty.

Signature

A signature which is placed very squarely in the middle of the available space can mean the writer wants special attention, and if a small name is expanded to fill a large space, all the more so.

Signature   *Signature*

Not surprisingly, a signature that climbs upwards shows lots of confidence and one that goes downwards reveals the opposite. If the name is written partly below the line then this person could need cheering up because they really do feel low. If the whole of the signature is above the line then this is one happy person! If the signature is a bit wobbly, the writer might be uptight, worried or excited.

Signature   *Signature*

✶⅄ LITTLE DETAILS

Very often the signature will have a little identifying mark or decoration and this may be connected to the person's profession. For instance, the rock star Bruce Springsteen (ask your Mum about him!) has a musical symbol in his signature, and the legendary footballer Pele had a little football!

Putting a full stop after your name means you place limits on yourself and may be very cautious. If the name is circled completely then the writer may be cut off and depressed, and if there is a line through the signature, as if it is being crossed out, then the person really does need to talk things through and to feel better about themselves. A very complex signature, with lots of flourishes and intertwining strokes can mean someone who wants to be important and who over-complicates anything and everything. It could also show someone who is going to great lengths to prevent forgery!

75

Someone who makes corrections to their signature lacks confidence and is generally not satisfied with themselves or with what they have achieved. If the signature is mainly straight and balanced, then this person is their own worst critic and may be very driven to excel.

It is a good idea to also look at the names within the signature and whether they are written in the same way. For instance, someone who writes their first name larger than their surname values their individuality more than their family – see Chapter four (page 40) for more on this.

A signature that just cannot be read means the writer doesn't care about being clear. If this is placed at the end of the letter, then either they aren't bothered about a reply or they are ashamed or embarrassed about what they have written.

Take a look at the zones in a signature. Some names give very little scope for an upper or lower zone. Teresa, for instance, has no lower zone naturally, and yet I always write it so that the downstroke of the 'T' goes well below the line,

Teresa Moorey

showing physical energy, pragmatism and determination to get to the root of things! Teresa Moorey is also an example of a name that has the minimum of opportunities for an emphasized upper case (there will always be at least two capitals in any full signature). I make the most of the 'T' and the 'M', writing them taller than the other letters, showing a spiritual and idealistic side, and a bit of the patronizing old 'Mother Hen' in the long 'T' bar that stretches over half of my first name!

* ⋆ ⋆

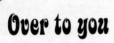

Over to you

How good are you at spotting the meanings of signatures? Take a look at the opposite four signatures and team them with the correct description of the writer.

Match the signatures

A A young person who has been in the police force for a year, who is energetic and impatient.

B A young person on a demanding course in Stage Management, who had to overcome dyslexia.

C A young person who gained First Class honours in Maths, Accountancy and Japanese and is now studying to be an actuary.

D A dramatic, confident young person who loves to be noticed.

HOW CONFIDENT ARE YOU?

1

2

3

4

Turn to pages 111–113 to see how many you got right.

CHAPTER EIGHT

Writing in colour

When you are writing in school you will usually have to use blue or black biro. But sometimes when writing in your own notebook or dashing off a note to a friend, you might like to write in another colour. You probably have a favourite, and this says a lot about your personality.

 Black
This is one of the 'standard' colours, blue being the other. If you choose black over blue you certainly know your own mind and you expect others to take you seriously. You are probably ambitious and see yourself one day as a high-flying executive. Choice of career is important to you.

Blue
Another 'normal' colour; if you prefer blue to black you are pleasant, co-operative and outgoing. You are warm and open, wanting to bring people close to you. Your standards are quite high – you don't like letting people down. Spiritual beliefs are important to you, and if you choose royal blue then you may have a vocation and want to help others.

 Turquoise
You may be able to write in turquoise in an exercise book at school – make sure you check first! If you use it you want to be just that bit different without being 'edgy' and you are probably artistic and creative as well.

 Pale blue
This colour shows sensitivity and artistic ability but you could get the 'blues' sometimes. Don't take life too seriously!

Green

If you choose to write in green when you can, then you're creative and quick-thinking. You've got lots of strings to your bow, you're imaginative and you have 'flair'. You don't want to be like everyone else – that's boring! But your self-esteem could maybe do with a boost sometimes.

Red

If you reach for the red pen, you've got attitude! You're very ambitious and your get-up-and-go is off the scale. You can be very generous and warm-hearted, but you can be a bit of a bossy know-it-all at times.

Pink

A bright pink is a bit like red, but softer – and the paler the pink the gentler the vibe. If you love to pen it in pink then you are friendly and like to get close. Sometimes you could make yourself a bit too vulnerable. If you choose a purply-pink you like to feel really special.

Go for it, but don't get too carried away. If you feel good writing in baby pink, then you might be too dependent on your friends – don't be afraid to strike out on your own sometimes.

Brown

This is a practical, reliable colour and if you choose it then you take life quite seriously and like people to see you as someone they can count on. But even though this is a dark 'sensible' colour, it's still out-of-the-ordinary. Your secret is that you like to impress.

Orange

If you grab an orange pen then you're cheerful, with a wonderful sense of humour and lots of energy. You look on the bright side and love to make everyone smile. You have lots of ideas but you don't always get around to putting them into practice.

83

Yellow

Using a yellow pen shows your mind is quick and you love to communicate – so there's a contradiction here, because yellow, unless it is very bright can be hard to read. If you like to use yellow, chances are you use it for headings and highlighting – your words are just too good to waste on an ink no-one can see properly!

Purple

Bring out the stretch limo – this writer likes to be a bit special! Your standards are very high and your opinion of yourself isn't far behind! That's fine – it's good to aim high, but make sure you give other people room, too.

Over to you

You will already know what colour you really like to write in and will have realized something more about yourself from this chapter. But whatever your preference, did you know that you can use coloured pens to change your mood? Even if you aren't very keen on a colour, it can still have the desired effect.

✧ Want to be more cheerful? Scrawl in ORANGE.

✧ Need to boost your self-esteem?
  Do some PURPLE flourishes.

✧ Want more get-up-and-go?
  Get out the RED pen.

✧ Want some flashes of inspiration?
  Get busy with a YELLOW highlighter.

✧ Need to come back to Planet Earth?
  Try a BROWN pen.

✧ Want to be kind and cuddly?
  PINK will bring out the girly you.

✧ Want to encourage your creativity?
  A GREEN pen will help.

✧ Need to chill out? Choose BLUE.

✧ Want to take control?
  Make your mark in BLACK.

Have fun! Why not treat yourself to some new
coloured pens and start to discover their power.

CHAPTER NINE

Properly addressed

Before reading this chapter, find an envelope and address it. Then you'll be able to find out things about yourself from the way you've gone about it. It's easy to alter the way you place an address if you secretly want to fit a certain description. If you have a pen pal, make sure you save her envelopes – the way she addresses them will tell you loads about her personality.

When people address letters, they are aware that they are creating an impression. Even though they probably don't know anything about graphology they do know that the person who receives the letter may notice how neat and pleasant the envelope looks. Because of this the address does tend to indicate more outward matters than what you find on the inside of the envelope. Rather like clothes, the address reflects the bits of the personality that are 'on show'.

To interpret an address you need to look at where it is placed on the envelope. Obviously some addresses take up more space than others but you should be able to get a basic idea.

Address placed in the middle
As long as it isn't cramped to fit a little 'box' this shows a sensible approach. The writer is organized, careful and likes to have an 'all-round' view of things before making decisions. This person's bedroom is probably really neat. They are generally thoughtful and clear-headed.

Address too low
The writer isn't a very happy person and often feels as if they have the weight of the world on their shoulders. They tend to expect the worst.

Address too high
'Look before you leap' is something this writer hasn't heard of! Still they probably aren't too bothered what scrapes they get into because they're in too much of a dream to notice! Practical considerations are the last things on their minds – if they've got wet feet and no cash they just won't notice if they've got interesting stuff to think about.

Address high and to the left
No party animal here! This writer prefers their own company and might not trust other people very much. They tend to get lost inside their own heads and don't like to come out of their shell to help people. They're probably scared of the future, too. If this is you – take a deep breath and relax!

Address high and to the right
This is a free spirit, maybe even a rebel. The writer has 'Attitude' with a capital 'A' and doesn't like to feel tied down or beholden to anyone. They like what they do to be as perfect as possible and they always aim high.

Address generally to the right
This person has strong feelings and looks to other people for support. They aren't keen on taking

the lead but they can't settle for long either. The wrong sort of crowd is bad news for this person, but supportive friends will make them feel great.

Address generally to the left
The writer keeps themself to themself, preferring one or two good friends to being with a crowd. No wearing the heart on the sleeve – this person plays their cards close to their chest and feels safer in the background.

Address low and to the left
The green-eyed monster is lurking here! The writer tends to suspect everyone and can feel envious and threatened. They like to hang on to their money, too. If this is you try to be aware that you may be making things worse for yourself by the attitude you are taking. Most people are okay – and don't underestimate yourself so much!

Address low and to the right
This person believes that the grass is always greener on the other side. They like the good things in life but they don't take chances. Everything has to be sewn up, and there's no pulling the wool over their eyes.

Address descends like 'steps' from the top left to bottom right
Here we have a cautious type who doesn't make friends easily. If this is you, you could be a bit too suspicious but at least you can keep out of trouble!

Address shows lots of flourishes
What you see isn't what you get – this person puts on a show but inside it's a different matter.

Address is very hard to read
You'll be lucky if you get this letter in the first place! Deep inside the writer isn't sure that he or she wants you to – they just don't like to be too ordinary and may have a lot of trouble communicating because of this. If this is you,

please remember that in order to be a real individual and a feisty personality, you don't have to be unco-operative!

Address is similar to the writing inside
This person is relaxed and doesn't put on an act – great! You'll know where you are with them.

Address is very different to the writing inside
It's no surprise that this person has a 'front'. Their real feelings may be hidden.

Address is underlined or really stands out
The sender may be the type to make mountains out of molehills. If this is you try not to waste effort and energy where it isn't needed. You'll achieve more if you target what is important.

Over to you

Got that envelope you addressed at the start of the chapter? What does it tell you about you? Do you agree? Most importantly, are you happy with it? If not, make up your mind to address envelopes differently in future.

Why not ask all your friends to send you a letter? Tell them it's a game for a sleepover, and they'll find out what when they come over. When you're all settled, get out the envelopes and check them against the interpretations in this chapter. See what you can discover!

Remember it's more fun and personal to receive and send a letter than it is to email or text. It's also a great way to practise your new graphology skills. What are you waiting for? Get scribbling!

CHAPTER TEN

How do you doodle?

All those squiggles down the side of your Maths homework mean more than that you're just bored! They speak volumes about what's really going on in your mind.

✱人 WHAT DO YOUR DOODLES SAY ABOUT YOU?

Hearts
Well ... it doesn't take a genius to work that one out! But it might not just be one special lad who's on your mind. Chances are you're kind and loving. Just make sure you look after yourself as well!

Curves and circles

You like to get along with people. You are prepared to make compromises and you are affectionate.

Animals and flowers

You love all living things and like to take care of them. You are gentle and friendly. You are probably a dreamer, and also like to cuddle up on the sofa. If you're drawing little houses and gardens with pretty trees, then you are a warm-hearted person who likes to make other people feel good.

Faces

You're a party animal and you like to be with the gang as much as you can. Looks and appearance are also very important to you. You like meeting new people – you're the one who volunteers to show people round the school or takes the new

pupil under your wing. It's important to you to be liked. If the face you draw looks to the left, the past is affecting you; if it looks to the right, you're future-orientated. But if the face has a nasty look then you're not

satisfied with life and often feel bad about things
– and you'd like someone to realize this!

Rectangles and squares

These reveal a practical and orderly
side to your nature. However, if there
are shapes inside the boxes then you
feel trapped and fenced in –
possibly emotionally.

Twists and tangles

You feel confused, 'in a mess' and torn two ways.
Give yourself time to sort out your head.

Numbers

If you are doodling the same number over and
over again, ask yourself what it means in your life.
Are you worried about money, thinking of
phoning someone or remembering an address?

Sharp shapes

Anything in your doodle that looks like
a weapon could mean that you are very
angry with someone. Try to express your
feelings in a positive way.

96

Spreading doodles
If your doodles try to take over the page and
are complicated and interesting, then you are
probably artistic and inventive. This is even more
likely if you can't resist doodling in colour!

Filled-in doodles
If your doodles have lots of areas that you have
shaded in, or where you have pressed very hard,
then you are probably very worried or scared
about something. You would like
more certainty in your life. Find
someone to talk to about your
feelings to get things in proportion.

In perspective
If your doodles are three-dimensional then you
are able to plan and think in a practical,
constructive way. You can think clearly and
quickly and are probably very bright.

Thin shapes
Unhappiness and repression are indicated by doodles that are thin and wavery, and look droopy, narrow or cramped. Possibly you are afraid of your feelings, or feel you have been deprived.

Cars and trains
Drawing anything that suggests travel means that you want to escape. If you have pressed very hard, then you really are desperate! Time to try and organize a holiday for yourself.

Same doodle over and over again
Your mind is like a broken record, playing the same track over and over again. Try to think about something else.

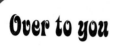

Over to you

Doodles can work both ways – if you consciously doodle certain shapes they can help to change your mood.

Doodle therapy

☆ **Want to come down to earth?**
Draw squares, but make sure there's nothing inside them.

☆ **Need to cheer up?**
Smiley faces will help.

☆ **Getting in the mood to party?**
Draw lots of smiley faces, with
ribbons and balloons.

☆ **Want to plan a great sleepover?**
Draw a house, with curtains at the windows and
a smoking chimney to get that welcoming vibe.

☆ **Being taken for a ride?**
Stop drawing hearts and flowers and draw some
sharp shapes – but don't get too angry!

☆ **Need some extra patience for a**
friend who's upset?
Draw furry animals and leafy plants.

☆ **Drumming up some creative ideas?**
Let yourself do a great big doodle, and fill the
page with colour.

☆ **Want to get top marks in a test?**
Draw a neat doodle in three dimensions i.e. so
it looks real and solid.

Doodle sleepover game

Every person playing will need two sheets of A4 paper, a pen and paperclip. Put your name at the top of the paper. Now everyone just relaxes and draws whatever they want on one sheet of paper – don't try to do a masterpiece, all that's needed is some interesting squiggles. Don't copy others just scribble whatever you want. Play your favourite music if you like. Time yourselves – five minutes is probably enough.

Now clip the doodle sheet to the plain sheet and pass to your neighbour on your left. She should write her first impressions of the doodle at the top of the blank page. There is no need to be clever, everyone should write whatever comes to mind. Fold the paper over so what has been written can't be seen and pass it to the left again. When the pages have gone round and everyone has their own doodle back again, look at all the comments. Do you agree? Check them out against what it says in this chapter – you may have come to similar conclusions.

This game can be interesting and revealing,
as well as a real laugh. Just don't take it too
seriously – always focus on the good stuff and
remember there's much more to you than your
doodles. If you do it with your friends you trust
and feel comfortable with it will be all the
more successful.

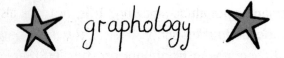

CHAPTER ELEVEN

Amazing you!

The great news about graphology is that it cuts both ways. If you make changes in your writing, eventually these changes will be reflected in your personality. Sounds amazing? It is, but it is also simple and makes sense.

There is a fascinating practice called biofeedback. It is a way of feeding information back to your body so it becomes more conscious of how it is working. A good example has been found in the case of people who have migraines. If the brain can get into a certain 'mood' where it generates 'alpha waves' then the migraine goes. But most of us can't do that at will – we aren't quite sure when we're making those waves. So scientists rigged people up to a machine that read brainwaves, and when the alpha waves came along, on came a light. Soon the people who had been connected to the machines learnt how to make the light come on. After that it wasn't long before they could make alpha waves without any machine checking up on them.

Changing your writing isn't quite like that, but it's similar. When you form a letter differently a message goes back to your brain telling it that what it feels corresponds to that letter-shape. This change in your writing sends a tiny nerve impulse back to your brain, which then reacts to that message. You could compare this to a lot of things that change your mood. For instance, if you take a deep breath it seems to calm you. A bigger effect might come from hearing a tune you really love. It makes you feel good, and if you dance to it you probably feel even better. If you do that several times a day you probably feel a more upbeat, cheerful person all round! The effects of changing your writing are more subtle, but they go deeper. Unconsciously you 'know' that the different writing means something about you, and your brain adapts accordingly.

Let's look at an example. After reading this
book you know that writing that slopes to the
right tends to be more extrovert than writing that
slants back, to the left. If you make your writing
slant more to the right, you will gradually become
more outgoing, wanting to be with the crowd as
much as you can. This would happen if you knew
nothing about graphology and were just told to
do it by a friend who could analyse handwriting.
Because you are 'in the know' you can choose
what you want to achieve and chances
are it will come about even quicker.

Can you make any changes at all? No, you can't
change your entire personality! Of course if you
were determined you could alter your writing
a great deal but this would spoil the flow and
make you stressed and uptight. Any changes you
make should be small and the writing should
come naturally.

More sociable
We've already seen that writing slope indicates
extroversion or the opposite. If your writing slopes

to the left and you would like to be more outgoing, try making it more upright and see what happens. Don't go too far and slope it miles to the right – just see how you feel after a couple of months of upright writing and take it from there.

Becoming tidier

If your folks are always going on at you about the state of your room, and your teacher says your

work is a mess, try dotting your 'i's and crossing your 't's – literally! The messages of neatness that this will send to your brain should make getting sorted much easier.

More down-to-earth

If you're a bit of a dreamer, your 't' bars may well be drifting above the uprights. Make sure you cross the 't' centrally and keep your writing on the line.

More get-up-and-go

If your writing lacks much in the way of a lower zone, try forming some nice, balanced loops under your 'g's, 'j's, 'p's and 'y's. Gradually you'll feel more energetic and be keen to take up new sports or activities.

Becoming more confident

If you are a bit of a shrinking violet, chances are you leave big right-hand margins, have tiny crosses on your 't's and your capital 'I' is cramped.

Try changing all of these – but be careful you don't go in for enormous 'I's because that also is a sign that you're not overly confident.

Less of a show-off

Just stop decorating your writing, especially capitals, with lots of flourishes and loops.

Able to keep a secret

To stop that motormouth, close the tops of your little 'a's and 'o's.

Better tempered

A short temper may be shown by angular writing and long dashes over 'i's instead of dots. Try to write in a more flowing, softer style and shorten the stroke over the 'i'.

Slow down!
If your 't' bar is ahead of the 't' to the right, then you probably jump to conclusions and your brain is always running ahead. Bring that 't' bar back where it belongs to slow yourself down.

More independence
Try writing small 's' in a printed manner, not the usual looped, joined-up version, especially at the end of words, and write capital 'M' separate from the following word.

More self-control
Watch out for loops on the upright stroke of small 't' – straighten this out and you'll be less emotional and sorry for yourself. If your writing slopes extremely to the right, try making it just a bit more upright.

More upbeat
If the line of your writing droops downwards, try to slope it upwards instead – you'll feel you're getting somewhere!

There are lots of ideas for you to try but PLEASE only try one, and keep it simple. Make up a good sentence that also expresses what you want to change and include the change in that sentence. For instance, if you want more confidence write, 'I am a confident, attractive person' ten times, making sure the 'I' is larger, stronger and straighter than in your usual script. Do this each day for two months at least, because it will take a while to alter the way you have been feeling. Soon you should notice a growing change in your personality. It's exciting to realize just how much power you have to shape your life!

Last words

Having worked through this book you are well on your way to being a graphologist. You have gained a deeper insight into people and lots of knowledge that you can share with your friends and family. Handwriting analysis proves that we are all totally unique. Be proud of your individuality, and proud of your handwriting which is proof of who you are deep inside.

If you really want to be an expert, carry on collecting samples of handwriting of people you know. Write down all you know of that person and see if you can see all their characteristics in their writing. You can study more advanced books, too, but remember that nothing can take the place of experience. And always be positive! There is something good in all of us and like all the mysterious arts, graphology is there to show us how to make the most of ourselves – to be truly and utterly amazing!

Answers to Match the signatures

A pairs with 2

Daniel's sharp, upward slanting 'D' indicates some aggression and ambition. His confidence is still developing so he only signs the initial of his first name. He does not complete his surname and he circles it suggesting he is protective of his past. Physical energy is shown by the hard pressure.

B pairs with 3

Jonathan has battled with dyslexia, shown in the careful formation of his surname. Very hard pressure shows plenty of energy for his demanding Stage Management course and the

arched formation of his letters show creativity.
Variable slope and the first name only initialled
reveal his individuality is yet to break through
into his signature.

C pairs with 4

Lucie's capital 'L' shows her involvement with
money and her slightly angular script a sharp
and quick mind. She gives prominence to her
first name showing self-development, but a loop
comes back from her surname indicating that
her past affects her. Like Daniel's signature,
Lucie's is protecting something and the line
through her name shows she could feel a bit
down at times. However, the overall upward
slant indicates optimism.

D pairs with 1

Samantha is dramatic and impatient! Her signature is composed of just two strokes, with a single curve to the 'S' showing a sensuous nature. Like Daniel's and Jonathan's signatures, she does not write out her first name, showing her individuality is still hidden, to some extent. However, the forward drive of her signature displays her determination to succeed, although she may not always finish things off.

As a matter of interest – Daniel and Jonathan are brothers, showing just how differently you can write a surname!

Index

addressing an envelope 87-93

angular writing 13, 27, 33, 107

boys x, 4, 26-27, 31-38, 94

brain and writing ix, 1, 70, 103, 104, 106

capital 'I' 67-70, 107, 109

careers 52, 53, 54, 55, 80

consciously changing your writing 70, 103, 105-109

crossing 't's 41, 44, 50, 64, 106, 107

doodles 94-102

dotting 'i's 26, 41, 42, 44, 47, 50, 64, 106, 107

family x, 39-51, 52, 55

fashion 62-66

figures in writing 43, 55-56, 69

first name 39, 40, 76, 77, 111, 112, 113

friends' writing x, 19-30, 67, 87, 93, 101

graphology
at work 3
history of 1-2

joined-up writing 10, 48, 50-51

left-handers 9-10

line of writing 11-12, 20, 32, 73, 74, 77

margins 20, 34-38, 107

money 6, 34, 35, 36, 42-43, 69, 90, 96, 112

narrow writing 20, 22, 24, 27, 32, 43, 50, 69

neat writing 14, 24, 41, 56, 64

separate writing 10, 50, 108

shape of writing 12-14

signatures 11, 40, 71-79, 111-113

size 11, 25, 45, 62, 50, 72, 73

slope 7-8, 12, 19, 20, 28, 48, 49, 52, 54, 63, 70, 105, 108, 112

surname 39, 40, 76, 111, 112, 113

three zones, the 5-7, 77
   lower zone 6, 7, 26, 31, 61, 77, 106
   middle zone 6, 26, 27, 32, 33, 49, 63
   upper zone 6, 25, 33, 64, 77

upright writing 8, 52, 54, 55, 56, 58, 65, 106

wide writing 19, 22, 43
writing
   and age 7, 48-49
   artistic 13, 51, 56, 81, 97
   creative 10, 51, 58, 81, 82, 100, 112
   in colour ix, 80-86
   literary 57-58, 69
   pressure 23-24, 32, 40, 58, 62, 64, 111
   speed 14-16